THE SEVEN LAST WORDS
FROM THE CROSS

Cambridge Hist
of med

Roy Porter

FLEMING RUTLEDGE

The Seven Last Words from the Cross

WILLIAM B. EERDMANS PUBLISHING COMPANY

GRAND RAPIDS, MICHIGAN / CAMBRIDGE, U.K.

Wm. B. Eerdmans Publishing Co.

255 Jefferson Ave. S.E., Grand Rapids, Michigan 49503 /
P.O. Box 163, Cambridge CB3 9PU U.K.

Printed in the United States of America

11 10 09 08 07 06   10 9 8 7 6 5 4

Library of Congress Cataloging-in-Publication Data

Rutledge, Fleming.
The seven last words from the cross / Fleming Rutledge.
          p.   cm.
Includes bibliographical references.
ISBN-10: 0-8028-2786-1
ISBN-13: 978-0-8028-2786-9 (pbk. : alk. paper)
1. Jesus Christ — Seven last words.   I. Title.

BT457.R88   2005
232.96′35 — dc22
                              2004056312

www.eerdmans.com

Dedicated with gratitude
to my beloved sister Betsy McColl,

who loves the Three Hours,

and who understands the reasons
this little book
is also dedicated
to the memory of
Theodore Parker Ferris

Contents

Author's Note

These meditations on the Seven Last Words of Christ from the Cross are revised and expanded versions of seven meditations delivered for the Good Friday Three Hours in two Episcopal churches: Trinity in Columbus, Georgia, 2002; and Trinity, Copley Square, Boston, 2003. Such opportunities on Good Friday are the high points of a lifetime spent in the pulpit. I am deeply grateful to both these congregations for the incomparable privilege of preaching at these services.

The prayerful singing of hymns, with special attention to the words, is a chief feature of such services. I have attempted to give the reader a sense of this experience by reproducing selected stanzas of certain hymns as devotional reflections on the seven meditations.

The Seven Words, or sayings, from the Cross are given in the traditional King James Version in the chapter headings. In the body of the text the KJV is less frequently used; I have chosen the Revised Standard Version for most quotations.

New York, Lent 2004   F.R.

*"Father, forgive them,
for they know not
what they do"*

Two others also, who were criminals, were led away to be put to death with him. And when they came to the place which is called The Skull, there they crucified him, and the criminals, one on the right and one on the left. And Jesus said, "Father, forgive them; for they know not what they do."

LUKE 23:32-34

For Christians, Good Friday is the crucial day, not only of the year but of world history. The source of the word *crucial* is significant. It comes from the Latin *crux*, meaning "cross." Here is Webster's definition of *crucial*: "Having the nature of a final choice or supreme trial; supremely critical; decisive." That conveys something of the unique character of this day. The early Christian apostles proclaimed the Cross and Resurrection of Jesus Christ to be the decisive turning point for all the ages of the created universe (Col. 1:15-20; Heb. 1:1-4). On this day we set aside our other concerns to meditate upon what this astonishing claim might mean.

The four New Testament Gospels record seven "words," or sayings, from the crucified Jesus of Nazareth. It has long been customary on Good Friday to preach seven meditations on the Seven Words. In the traditional order, the first saying is from the Gospel of Luke: "Father, forgive them, for they know not what they do." In order to enter into this saying, we need to reflect on what is being forgiven.

Good Friday is an unrelenting day. It is unrelenting like the regimes of Pol Pot, Idi Amin, Saddam Hussein, and many, many others who throughout human history have mercilessly put people to death by torture. We in twenty-first-century America are shocked and horrified to hear of the terrible things that were done to people in the dungeons of men like Saddam. We can scarcely imagine these things, living as we do in a country where inhuman behavior is against the law.

In Jesus' time, crucifixion was not against the law. It was carried out *by* the law. It was an exceptionally gruesome method of torturing a person to death, carried out by the government not in secret dungeons but in public. Not even the celebrated film by Mel Gibson, *The Passion of the Christ,* can convey the full ghastliness of crucifixion to a modern audience. We don't understand it because we have never seen anything like it in the flesh. The situation was very different in New Testament times. Everybody had seen crucified men along the roadsides of the Roman Empire. Everyone knew what it looked like, smelled like, sounded like — the horrific sight of completely naked men in agony, the smell and sight of their bodily functions taking place in full view of all, the sounds of their groans and labored breathing going on for hours and, in some cases, for days. Perhaps worst of all is the fact that no one cared. All of this took place in public, and no one cared. That is why, from the early Christian era, a verse from the book of Lamentations was attached to the

Good Friday scene: "Is it nothing to you, all you who pass by?" (1:12).

For Jews and Gentiles alike in those days, a crucified person was as low and despised as it was possible to be. Crucifixion sent an unmistakable signal: this person that you see before you is not fit to live, not even human (as the Romans put it, such a person was *damnatio ad bestias,* meaning "condemned to the death of a beast" — although in our society it would be considered unacceptable to kill even an animal in such a way). There was nothing religious, nothing uplifting or inspiring about a crucifixion. On the contrary, it was deliberately intended to be *obscene,* in the original sense of that word; the Oxford English Dictionary suggests "disgusting, repulsive, filthy, foul, abominable, loathsome." It is therefore of the utmost importance to note that in an era when crucifixion was still going on and was widely practiced throughout the Roman Empire, Christians were proclaiming a degraded, condemned, *crucified person* as the Son of God and Savior of the world. By any ordinary standard, and especially by religious standards, this was simply unthinkable. Here is one of the most powerful arguments for the truth of the Christian faith: the human religious imagination could not have arrived at a notion so utterly

———

foreign to generally accepted spiritual ideas as that of a crucified Messiah.

We are so accustomed to seeing crosses, wearing them on chains, carrying them in processions, and so forth, that it is almost impossible to grasp their original horror. We are accustomed to thinking of the Cross merely as a "religious symbol," like the Star of David or the yin-yang. Yet at the most fundamental level — this can't be emphasized strongly enough — the Cross is in no way "religious." This is very hard for us to understand today. Over time, we have developed ways of romanticizing violent death so as to make it seem spiritual and inspiring. Cruel methods of execution such as burning at the stake have been sanctified over the generations so that they appear "religious"; Joan of Arc, for example, is depicted in the flames with her eyes uplifted in holy awe. The typical "religious" Easter card shows the Cross in a soft, flattering light, surrounded by lilies; you would never know that it was originally an instrument of extreme brutality. We need to make a conscious effort to understand that the Cross in reality is, by a very long way, the most *irreligious, unspiritual* object ever to find its way into the heart of faith. This fact is a powerful testimony to the unique significance of the death of Christ.

———

Now that we have *The Passion of the Christ*, for better and worse, it is not as necessary as it once was to spell out the peculiar horror of crucifixion for modern audiences. Not even this film can depict its full ghastliness, however, because we are always aware that it is not "real." In any case, Mr. Gibson pays more exquisite attention to the scourging than to the crucifixion itself.

What we need to reflect upon today is the striking fact that the Four Evangelists tell us nothing at all about Christ's physical suffering. Why is that? It must be because they want to emphasize something else. It is our role, this Good Friday, to try to understand what that is. Perhaps we can do so by reflecting upon recent conflicts. We have been reminded more than once lately that it is against the Geneva Conventions to display or humiliate a POW. Crucifixion, however, was purposefully designed to do just that — to display and to humiliate. The crosses were placed by the roadside as a form of public announcement: these miserable beings that you see before you are not of the same species as the rest of us. The purpose of pinning the victims up like insects was to invite the gratuitous abuse of the passersby. Those crowds understood that their role was to increase, by jeering and mocking, the degradation of those who had been thus designated unfit to live. The theological meaning of this is that crucifixion is an enactment of the worst that we are, an embodiment of the most sadistic and inhuman impulses that lie within us. The Son of God absorbed all that, drew it into himself. All the cruelty of the human race came to focus in him.

The historian Peter Brown has noted that the New Testament shows us life lived between two worlds, the Roman and the Near Eastern cultures.[1] Crucifixion was noxious enough in Roman eyes; Palestinian attitudes would have found it perhaps even more so. Near Eastern cultures had, and still have, "an acute sense of personal honor lodged in the body." An amputation administered as punishment, for instance, would be seen as much more than just physical cruelty or permanent handicap; it would mean that the amputee would carry the visible marks of dishonor and shame for the rest of his or her life. Anything done to the body would have been understood as exceptionally cruel, not just because it inflicted pain but even more because it caused dishonor. And so the Passion accounts reflect, in part, "a very ancient ritual

1. We say "Middle East" today, but when scholars speak or write of the area in Jesus' time, it is "the ancient Near East."

of humiliation." The mocking of Jesus, the spitting and scorn, the "inversion of his kingship," the "studious dethronement" with the crown of thorns and purple robe — all were part of a deliberate procedure of shaming that unfolded in several stages, of which the crucifixion itself was only the culmination.[2]

Some of the most arresting paintings of the mockery of Jesus are unsparing in their depiction of the sheer viciousness and inhumanity of the men torturing him. We see in their faces the twisted expressions of those who have lynched black people. We see the sadistic glee of those who have abused prisoners of war. We see the uncanny smiles reported to have been on the faces of the terrorist pilots who struck the World Trade Center. And if we are truly honest with ourselves this Good Friday, we see also *within our own hearts* the capacity, under certain circumstances, to engage in terrible acts, or to assign others to do terrible acts in our name while we wash our hands of them. During the Iraq war in 2002, a military chaplain preached a homily to a little congregation of U.S. troops in the southern Iraqi desert, and this is what he said: "We still have some enemies to deal with. En-

2. Conversation with Peter Brown, Princeton, 1999.

---

emies. Truth be told, a lot of our enemies are not up north. *A lot of our enemies are here, in the heart.*"[3]

You have heard the saying "He is his own worst enemy." But that is a patronizing thing that people say loftily about *others,* not realizing that we are *all* our own worst enemy. This meditation will be followed by a hymn, "Beneath the Cross of Jesus." (Part of the importance of these meditations is the use of the hymns as personal devotions, paying special attention to the words.) The last verse of this hymn says that we "let [our] pride go by." This means that we will let go of pretense, acknowledging that an enemy lodges not only in the hearts of those whom we like to call the "bad guys," but also in our own hearts.

In this same hymn, there is a line reading, "My sinful self my only *shame,* my glory all the cross." The word *shame* is central to the meaning here. Crucifixion was *shameful.* The Epistle to the Hebrews puts special emphasis on this, saying that our Lord "endured the cross, despising the shame" (Heb. 12:2). Yet Jesus of all people did not deserve to be shamed. Whose shame is it, then? "My

3. Michael Wilson, "Protecting the Rear in 100 Degree Heat," *The New York Times,* 6 April 2003 (italics added).

sinful self *my* only shame." It is *our* shame that we see Jesus taking upon himself. In the mocking of Jesus, in his death by torture, we see all of the absolute worst that people can do. And here is what we need to remember. In this first word from the Cross, Jesus does not pray for the good and the innocent. He prays for people doing terrible things. He prays for men who are committing sadistic acts, offering them to his Father's mercy. It is for his enemies that he prays, saying, "Father, forgive them, for they know not what they do."

There is a suggestion here that human beings are in the grip of something they do not fully comprehend. The evil that lodges in the human heart is greater than we know. This means at least two things. It means that there is nothing that you or I could ever do, or say, or be, that would put us beyond the reach of Jesus' prayers. Nothing at all. And it also means that no one else, no one at all, is beyond that reach. His prayer for the worst of the worst comes from a place beyond human understanding. From that sphere of divine power we hear these words today as though they were spoken for the first time, as though they were being spoken at this very moment by the living Spirit, spoken of each one of us: *Father, forgive them, for they know not what they do.*

Beneath the cross of Jesus I fain would take my stand,
The shadow of a mighty rock within a weary land,
A home within the wilderness, a rest upon the way,
From the burning of the noontide heat and the burden
        of the day.

Upon the cross of Jesus mine eyes at times can see
The very dying form of one who suffered there for me;
And from my smitten heart with tears two wonders
        I confess:
The wonders of redeeming love and my unworthiness.

I take, O cross, thy shadow for my abiding place;
I ask no other sunshine than the sunshine of his face;
Content to let my pride go by, to know no gain nor loss,
My sinful self my only shame, my glory all the cross.[4]

FIRST MEDITATION

4. Hymn 498 (Episcopal *Hymnal 1982*), "Beneath the Cross of Jesus," words by Elizabeth Cecilia Clephane (1830-1869), alt.

———

"Verily I say unto thee,
today thou shalt be with
me in Paradise"

Two others also, who were criminals, were led away to be put to death with him. And when they came to the place which is called The Skull, there they crucified him, and the criminals, one on the right and one on the left. . . . One of the criminals who were hanged railed at him, saying, "Are you not the Christ? Save yourself and us!" But the other . . . said, "Jesus, remember me when you come into your kingdom." And he said to him, "Truly, I say to you, today you will be with me in Paradise."

LUKE 23:32-33, 39-43

Crucifixion was for the scum of the earth. It was for what we call "common criminals." Uncommon criminals, white-collar criminals from privileged backgrounds with influential connections, would never have been crucified. This is very important for us to reflect upon. Jesus did exactly the opposite of what you and I would do. We want to get away from the dregs of human society. Jesus voluntarily became a part of the dregs himself.

I remember talking to a man from Eastern Europe who was painting our house in our suburban town. He was upset about what was happening to his neighborhood. He said that there was a "bad element" moving in. The phrase stayed with me. What he meant was that the new neighbors were a different color and spoke a different language. How quickly we all assign our fellow human beings to the category of "bad element." I am not immune to this. The trains I ride to New York City are no longer filled with the African-Americans that I have known all my life; now the passengers are Spanish-speaking laborers. To offset my feelings of estrangement, I try to imagine their stories — how they have suffered hardships to come to America, how they work long, hard hours and live in squalid conditions so they can send small sums back home to their wives and children. If one of them gets into trouble, he can't call his friend the lawyer, he can't drop the name of his neighbor the judge, he doesn't know anyone with enough money to post bail for him.

Throughout his life, Jesus aligned himself with the "bad elements." In his death, it was the same: he was crucified between two "malefactors," two wrongdoers. You have probably heard the familiar saying that Jesus was crucified not on the altar between two candles but on Golgotha between two thieves. That's a good saying, isn't it? But it doesn't go quite far enough, because they weren't just thieves. According to Mark and Matthew, they were worse than mere thieves; they were *bandits,* armed robbers, men of violence, prepared to kill as well as steal. This indeed is an "element" wildly unsuited to be in proximity to the divine. Good Friday summons us to think deeply about the profoundly strange, incongruous — indeed, unacceptable — nature of a crucified God nailed up between two bandits for the scorn of the passersby. Would you in a million years ever have dreamed of having such an objectionable fact at the heart of your faith? No such image of God has ever been imagined in all the history of religion. No one has ever

———

matched this story for sheer perversity — the divine re-deemer "defiled and put to scorn," in the words of our next hymn, obscenely displayed, reviled, mocked, spat upon, beaten nearly to death, naked, plagued by insects, covered with dirt and sweat and blood and excrement. This deeply troubling picture calls for interpretation. It calls for explanation. Why has the Son of God come to this end? It is our purpose, during these meditations, to enter more deeply into this crucial matter.

All four Evangelists — Matthew, Mark, Luke, and John — want us to know about the two malefactors on either side of our Lord. It seems to be a very deep part of the tradition about him. For one thing, it was prophesied in the Old Testament: Isaiah wrote, "he was numbered among the transgressors" (53:12). He was not numbered among the members of the religious establishment. He was not numbered among the politically connected. He was not numbered among the good, upstanding pillars of the community, the civic leaders or the business leaders or the church leaders. He was "numbered among the transgressors," for only "bad elements" were crucified. Jesus suffered "outside the city wall," away from the good neighborhoods, beyond the pale, cast out from the company of decent people. He was "numbered among the transgressors."

When I think of such things, I am reminded of someone I admire: Virginia Durr, a privileged Alabamian who during her entire girlhood never had to wonder for a single moment whether she belonged or not. She was a member of the "magic circle" of upper-class white society, a debutante and all that goes with it. She grew up to be the woman who, together with her husband, went down to the police station in Montgomery to bail out Rosa Parks on that famous night when the bus boycott began, and nothing in the segregated South was ever the same again. After that, Clifford Durr lost his law practice, and much of white Montgomery stopped speaking to them. Mrs. Durr's autobiography is called *Outside the Magic Circle*.[1] The Durrs took upon themselves the burden of the Son of God, who came to live among us as one outside the magic circle. Entering into the Good Friday Three Hours is to step outside with him for a space, "outside the camp" (Heb. 13:13) where the "best people" never go.

Now, the evangelist Luke, who gives us details about

1. Mrs. Durr's letters have recently been published. See *Freedom Writer: Virginia Foster Durr's Letters from the Civil Rights Years*, ed. Patricia Sullivan (New York: Routledge, 2003).

the two bandits and what they said to Jesus, intends for *us* to be drawn into the story. We are invited to see *ourselves* in these two malefactors. There are aspects of us in both of them, first one and then the other. Listen to this. We are like the one on the left: we say, "If you are the Messiah, save yourself — and save us too, while you're at it." Like this thief, we do not see any sign of Jesus' power in this crucifixion. How could the Son of God allow himself to be caught in this horrible situation? Most of us would not want to be connected to anything so shameful. For us the Cross can be a very ambiguous sign — a sign of weakness, ugliness, failure, incomprehension. Let us frankly acknowledge that we do not entirely like the Cross. That's why there will be so many more people in church on Easter Sunday than there are on Good Friday. We would rather have the glory of springtime than the glory of the Cross.

But what was that line from the hymn we read earlier? "My sinful self my only shame, my *glory* all the cross." Like the man on Jesus' right hand, you may find yourself blessed this noon hour, blessed by seeing glory where others can see nothing but a hideous scene of helplessness, torment, and death. What was it that the second malefactor saw in Jesus? Picture it for a moment: we have before us, on three crosses, three men in the same ghastly predicament with nothing to distinguish one from another except the mocking placard above Jesus' head that said "The King of the Jews." What did the second man see in that dying, tortured face? What sort of kingship did he glimpse there? Did he perhaps hear Jesus say, "Father, forgive them"? What do *you* see in the crucified figure before you today? What do you see?

"Jesus, remember me when you come into your kingdom." That is what the second thief said. In the Old Testament, when God "remembers," it has a distinct meaning. It does not mean "to think about" or "to recall to mind." That would not mean very much. When God "remembers," he does not just *think about* us. He *acts for* us, with power to save. Somehow the crucified criminal on Jesus' right was enabled to see something that day that no one else saw. He saw Jesus reigning as a King and determining the destinies of people even in his tormented and dying state. To see him that way, Luke is telling us, is to see him as he truly is and to understand the source of his power. Not by signs and wonders, not by magic and dazzlement, not by "shock and awe," but only by an ultimate act of God's own self-sacrifice does

Christ rule. His power is made known only through his death.

I ask you now: Can you see yourself as one for whom Jesus died? Can you say with the second thief, *Jesus, remember me when you come into your kingdom?* It was not only for the bandits and "bad elements" on the other side of the civilized divide; it was for us too, with our masks of innocence and our delusions about our own righteousness. His death was for us too. The next hymn gives us an opportunity to enter more deeply into a personal understanding of his self-offering for us. As the words open us up to the power of his death, we are assured of the gift of his life, a life which can begin to work in us *today*. As his life takes root in us, we will come to understand more and more how it is that God has assigned infinite value to all the "elements" of humanity. We will rejoice not only for ourselves but also for all those others who by human standards would not have been considered salvageable but are now promised an eternal destiny of joy with Christ in his heavenly Kingdom. *Today thou shalt be with me in Paradise.*

*   *   *

O sacred head, sore wounded, defiled and put to scorn;
O kingly head, surrounded with mocking crown of thorn:
What sorrow mars thy grandeur? Can death thy
      bloom deflower?
O countenance whose splendor the hosts of heaven adore!

Thy beauty, long-desirèd, hath vanished from our sight;
Thy power is all expirèd, and quenched the light of light.
Ah me! for whom thou diest, hide not so far thy grace:
Show me, O Love most highest, the brightness of thy face.

In thy most bitter passion my heart to share doth cry,
With thee for my salvation upon the cross to die.
Ah, keep my heart thus movèd to stand thy cross beneath,
To mourn thee, well-beloved, yet thank thee for thy death.

What language shall I borrow to thank thee,
      dearest Friend,
For this thy dying sorrow, thy pity without end?
Oh, make me thine forever! And should I fainting be,
Lord, let me never, never outlive my love for thee.

My days are few, O fail not, with thine immortal power,
To hold me that I quail not in death's most fearful hour;

That I may fight befriended, and see in my last strife
To me thine arms extended upon the cross of life.[2]

SECOND MEDITATION

2. Hymn 168 (Episcopal *Hymnal 1982*), "O Sacred Head, Sore Wounded," words by Paulus Gerhardt (1607-1676); stanzas 1-3 and 5 translated by Robert Seymour Bridges (1844-1930); stanza 4 translated by James Waddell Alexander (1804-1859), alt.

❧ THIRD MEDITATION ❧

*"Woman, behold thy son! . . .
Behold thy mother!"*

But standing by the cross of Jesus were his mother, and his mother's sister, Mary the wife of Clopas, and Mary Magdalene. When Jesus saw his mother, and the disciple whom he loved standing near, he said to his mother, "Woman, behold, your son!" Then he said to the disciple, "Behold, your mother!" And from that hour the disciple took her to his own home.

JOHN 19:25-27

As I travel around the country on my preaching rounds, I learn a lot about the church. Once, during Holy Week, I stayed with a husband and wife who, like me, were in their late middle age. A young woman named Luba was living with them. While I was there, I learned her story. She was a young Pentecostal Christian from the Ukraine who had been brought to America as a child in the 1980s to escape Communist oppression. The grandfather of the family had been imprisoned for his Christian faith; the parents and their children had lived in mortal dread that their Bibles would be taken away from them. They arrived in America with one suitcase apiece and no English at all except one phrase: "Thank you very much." They settled in Pittsburgh with freedom to worship openly in the Slavic Pentecostal Church there.

Later, Luba traveled to another American city to be a baby-sitter for a few weeks, and during that time my hosts observed not only her quiet intelligence and skill with the neighbors' children but also her developing Christian faith. They invited her to come and live with them and go to college, an opportunity she might otherwise never have had. By the time I met her, she had become like their adopted daughter.

Here is another story. In the 1990s I was invited to

preach in a Roman Catholic Church in Greenwich Village. I stayed four days and nights in the spacious, comfortable rectory. Every day I ate a sumptuous meal, with wine, at the rectory table. This repast was prepared and served by cheerful, energetic women who would have been named Bridget and Eileen a generation ago, but today are named Carmela and Pilar. I don't know when I have ever enjoyed anything more than those lunches with the priests and nuns in that rectory. There was a continual stream of bishops and teachers and clergy coming in to spend a few days or weeks — from Ireland, from Italy, from the Philippines. The conversation ranged back and forth between high theological matters and joyous story-telling. I felt that I was part of them and they were part of me. It was really amazing. Here I was, an ordained Protestant woman, yet made to feel perfectly at ease. It felt like the Kingdom of heaven to me. I will carry that memory around with me to the end of my days. My heart aches for the pain of the Catholic Church today. The Protestant churches are not free from these same sins. May God deliver the whole Church of Christ from the bonds of sin, both the sins of commission and the sins of overlooking and excusing those commissions.

But now what do these stories about Luba and the

---

lunches in the Catholic rectory have to do with the third saying from the Cross? Saint John tells us that Jesus, looking down from the Cross, said to his mother, "Woman, behold thy son!" And to the Beloved Disciple standing with her he said, "Behold thy mother!" And, from that moment, "he took her to himself."

Virtually everyone who is reading these words has probably heard this saying from the Cross interpreted in the following way:

- Jesus cared deeply for his mother.
- Jesus was worried about his mother's future.
- The saying therefore illustrates Jesus' love for his mother and his dying concern for her welfare.
- We are thereby instructed to take care of our own mothers.

Indeed, this interpretation goes as far back as Saint Augustine in the fourth century.[1]

However, this way of understanding the saying has long been considered insufficient by many other inter-

1. Augustine, it must be said, had an extremely convoluted relationship with his own mother, Saint Monica.

preters. It does not seem to fit the theology of John's Gospel at all, nor does it seem to suit the concerns of John's Passion narrative. In all of John's Gospel, the mother of Jesus is mentioned only twice, and her name, Mary, is never mentioned.[2] Because of Luke's Gospel, we think of Mary, the mother of Jesus, as a very particular human being with a distinct personality, but that is not the way the Fourth Gospel portrays her. In John's Gospel, she plays a *symbolic* role. In both her Johannine appearances, here and at the marriage at Cana in Galilee, Jesus calls her "Woman." In English, this sounds very rude, but in Jesus' culture it was perfectly correct for a man to address a woman that way. For instance, Jesus addresses the Samaritan woman at the well in this fashion in the fourth chapter (John 4:21). It is not, however, the way a man would address his mother.[3] So there is something more at stake here. Good Friday is not the first Mother's Day.

In the Greek, we are told that the Beloved Disciple, traditionally called John, took the mother of Jesus to

2. There is also a passing, inconsequential reference to her in John 2:12.

3. Much of this paragraph is based on Raymond E. Brown, *The Death of the Messiah: From Gethsemane to the Grave*, 2 vols., Anchor Bible Reference Library (New York: Doubleday, 1994), pp. 1019-26.

---

himself that very hour, or that he — in a literal transla-
tion — took her "*to his own* that very hour." Various Bible
translations say that he took her "to his own *home*," but
that isn't in the original text. If you have been to Ephesus,
in Asia Minor, you can see a house where John is supposed to have brought Mary to live with him after the
Resurrection, even though there is not the slightest evi-
dence of it. This interpretation is now generally agreed to
have little or no foundation in the text of the Gospel of
John.[4] What is actually happening in this word from the
Cross is much more significant for us on this very day
than we might have realized. The saying is not about being nice to your mother. It is about the new community
that comes into being through the power of Jesus.

We very often hear people say that they can be religious without coming to church. We hear people say that
their "community" is their support group, or their social
group, or even their political action group. Soldiers have
their platoons; firemen have their firehouses. We hear

---

4. A group of Roman Catholic and Protestant scholars have
agreed that the "mother of Jesus" in this Johannine passage is not
functioning like the later Mary of Roman Catholic devotion. See *Mary
in the New Testament*, ed. R. E. Brown, K. P. Donfried, et al. (Philadelphia: Fortress Press/New York: Paulist Press, 1978), pp. 206-18.

people railing against "the institutional church," and God knows that the church has stained her own robes so badly that we can only repent in dust and ashes. But the Christian community has a quality that the critiques do not take into consideration. When the Christian community is working the way it is *supposed* to, people are brought together who have absolutely nothing in common, who may have diametrically different views on things, who may even actively dislike each other. The Christian community, when it is not grieving the Holy Spirit, comes into being without regard to differences. Personal likes and dislikes have nothing to do with the body of Christ. "There is neither Jew nor Greek, there is neither slave nor free, there is neither male nor female; for you are all one in Christ Jesus" (Gal. 3:28).

By rewriting the covenant in his own blood, Jesus has done something completely new. In giving his mother to the disciple, he is causing a new relationship to come into existence that did not exist before. The disciple and the woman are not individual people here. They are symbolic: they represent the way that *family* ties are transcended in the church by *the ties of the Spirit*. That is why Jesus calls his mother "woman" in the Gospel of John. He is setting aside the blood relationship in order to create a much wider family. A story in Mark's Gospel makes the same point in a different way: "A crowd was sitting about [Jesus]; and they said to him, 'Your mother and your brothers are outside, asking for you.' And he replied, 'Who are my mother and my brothers?' And looking around on those who sat about him, he said, 'Here are my mother and my brothers!'" (Mark 3:32-34). So again, we see that Jesus is calling people into a new relationship with him and with one another. It is not that he has no room for his own family. We are not recommending that anyone be like the missionary who is so frenzied in his evangelistic endeavors that he ignores his wife and children. What we do see happening here, however, is that mothers and fathers and cousins and sisters are newly created by the Spirit of Christ where there is no blood relationship whatever, and sometimes no obvious similarity or even affection. It is *the new covenant* written in the blood of Jesus.

There will always be sin in the church until Christ comes again. But there are signs that we can identify, signs that new families in Christ are being created all the time. May his blessed Holy Spirit come afresh upon all the branches of his church here in this great country of America, where God has been pleased to bring members of all the peoples of the earth. May we who belong to Christ be newly committed to our calling, so that blood and race and class and theological differences may be truly transcended in his Name, for our good and for his glory.

*   *   *

The Church's one foundation is Jesus Christ her Lord;
She is his new creation by water and the Word:
From heaven he came and sought her to be his holy Bride;
With his own blood he bought her, and for her life
   he died.[5]

THIRD MEDITATION

5. Hymn 525 (Episcopal *Hymnal 1982*), "The Church's One Foundation," words by Samuel John Stone (1839-1900).

———

*"My God, my God,
why hast thou forsaken me?"*

And when the sixth hour had come, there was darkness over the whole land until the ninth hour. And at the ninth hour Jesus cried with a loud voice, "Eloi, Eloi, lama sabachthani?" which means, "My God, my God, why hast thou forsaken me?" And some of the bystanders hearing it said, "Behold, he is calling Elijah." And one ran and, filling a sponge full of vinegar, put it on a reed and gave it to him to drink, saying, "Wait, let us see whether Elijah will come to take him down." And Jesus uttered a loud cry, and breathed his last. And the curtain of the temple was torn in two, from top to bottom. And when the centurion, who stood facing him, saw that he thus breathed his last, he said, "Truly this man was the Son of God!"

MARK 15:33-39
(*see also* MATTHEW 27:45-54)

"My God, my God, why hast thou forsaken me?" Believe it or not, this saying from the Cross is the saying to have if you're having only one. It is the only one reported by two different Evangelists, Mark and Matthew. There have long been groups of Christians for whom this Cry of Dereliction is the central saying. It is the saying that "causes us to tremble," but rightly understood, it is also the saying that brings the most comfort, because it plumbs the most profound depths.

The *St. Matthew Passion* of J. S. Bach contains a remarkable feature which apparently is Bach's own invention. He puts a "halo" of strings around the sayings of Jesus. A musicologist says that this halo "floats round the utterances of Christ like a glory." Bach was the only composer of his time to see that the one right place to withdraw the "halo" was at the Cry of Dereliction — *Eloi, Eloi, lama sabachthani*. The glory of the Father was removed from the abandoned figure on the Cross. In his study of Bach's music, Jaroslav Pelikan writes, "There is a 'halo' for Christ's prediction of the crucifixion at the very beginning of the narrative, and for his prediction of the betrayal, and for every statement of his after that . . . *but now he is all alone and forsaken.*"[1]

---

1. Jaroslav Pelikan, *Bach Among the Theologians* (Philadelphia: Fortress Press, 1986), emphasis added.

The writer Nicholson Baker describes a little American girl with the odd name of Nory, who is living with her parents in Ely, in England. The town is dominated by its famous cathedral, arranged in the shape of a crucifixion because Jesus died upon the Cross. Nory wonders, "Why do they have to concentrate on the awful way he died?"[2] What wisdom is in that question! When most of us look at a cathedral, the last thing we are thinking about is the Cross. We are thinking about how beautiful and spiritual it is. Nory, however, has the right idea. We have already observed that crucifixion itself, an "utterly vile" method of putting someone to death, was far worse than any of us are presently capable of fully imagining, even if we were to see a graphic film. If it were fully depicted, we would be unable to look for very long. It is important to ask ourselves why Christ died in such an obscenely barbarous fashion. Why not poison, like Socrates, or a nice sharp sword, like Anne Boleyn? Even hanging would at least have been comparatively quick. The Gospel writers, however, do not dwell on these matters. Apparently they must have wanted us to focus on something else. That "some-

2. Nicholson Baker, *The Everlasting Story of Nory* (New York: Random House, 1998).

thing else" is found especially in the Cry of Dereliction. In this saying we find the closest thing to an answer to the question, "Why do they have to concentrate on the awful way he died?"

Let us attend to a reading from the Epistle of Saint Paul to the congregation in Galatia:

> For all who rely on works of the law are under a curse; for it is written, "Cursed be every one who does not abide by all things written in the book of the law, and do them." Now it is evident that no man is justified before God by the law; for "He who through faith is righteous shall live"; but the law does not rest on faith, for "He who does them shall live by them." Christ redeemed us from the curse of the law, having become a curse for us — for it is written, "Cursed be every one who hangs on a tree" — that in Christ Jesus the blessing of Abraham might come upon the Gentiles, that we might receive the promise of the Spirit through faith. (Gal. 3:10-14)

"Christ became accursed for us." There is a connection between "the awful way he died" and these verses from

---

Paul's letter. A crucified person in occupied Palestine was doubly accursed, both by the secular government and by the religious authorities. He was accursed in the *secular* sense because he was handed over to the curses of the population. They were *supposed* to curse at him; that was understood. Heaping abuse on a crucified person was part of the ritual, part of the entertainment.

During the Iraq war in 2003 there were some shocking photographs of a wounded Kurdish man in northern Iraq. He had been brought on a stretcher to the doors of a hospital. The hospital was refusing to take him in, and the Arab men standing by were spitting on him — spitting on a helpless, wounded man lying in pain. They did not even know who he was; but he was a member of the wrong group, so they were spitting on him. One of the photographs showed this.[3] Of course, nothing like that would ever happen in innocent, virtuous America ... unless perhaps the object of the spitting and cursing was a child molester, or a serial killer, or Susan Smith, who drowned her own small sons.[4] Or maybe some American immigrant with the unfortu-

3. Photograph by Ruth Fremson, *The New York Times*, 14 April 2003.
4. At the time of her incarceration, Susan Smith was cursed by spitting bystanders.

nate first name of Osama. Another news story told of a middle-class Muslim family from Jordan, living in Queens as official permanent residents of the United States. The oldest son was in the Navy, serving on the USS *Abraham Lincoln*. A younger son, age twelve, was being persecuted at his public school. Classmates jumped on him and told him they hoped his brother would come back dead.[5] Jesus, in his death, takes the part of all those who suffer from the curses of others.

A crucified person was also accursed in a *religious* sense. Saint Paul, one of the greatest minds ever to grapple with the Hebrew Scriptures, had thought long and hard about this. He pondered a text from Deuteronomy (21:23) which stated that a dead body left hanging on a tree was cursed by God. This posed a vexing dilemma for Paul, a conspicuously devout student of the Torah. How could the Messiah of Israel be crucified on a tree and cursed by God? How could the risen Christ who had knocked him off his horse and blinded him with his glory on the road to Damascus be the same as the one who was publicly declared to be God-forsaken? Was this

5. Daniel J. Wakin, "Fear for Navy Son and Fellow Muslims," *The New York Times*, 12 April 2003.

not an internal contradiction of the most serious sort? How could the death of Paul's Lord Jesus on a cross be reconciled with this clear passage in the Torah? Should the Deuteronomic verse just be declared an obsolete relic? Or did it perhaps hold a key to the problem of "the awful way he died"?

For many centuries — about eighteen centuries, to be exact — Christians believed that there was such a thing as Sin. Using this word with a capital "S" is a way of indicating that Sin is not a misdeed here and a misdeed there, but an autonomous, enslaving Power. The Apostle Paul is very clear about this: "All human beings," he writes, "both Jews and Greeks, are under the power of sin" (Rom. 3:9). In our own time, however, we have done our best to get rid of this idea. Much of the language about Sin has been removed from the Episcopal Prayer Book. We do not want to hear the older words telling how we are "tied and bound by the chain of our sins." We do not want to think of ourselves as sinners in such explicit terms.

It is particularly difficult for Christians to think of themselves this way during wartime. It is characteristic of people who are in a conflict to think of themselves as exclusively in the right. Anyone watching the cable news channels during a war would think that the course of the whole world depended upon heroic Americans fighting unredeemable evil. I believe that people who put themselves through a series of Good Friday meditations are willing and able to see that the picture is more ambiguous than that. Why do the wars never stop? Why do parents teach their children who they are supposed to hate, and then they teach their children, and then they teach theirs, world without end? Why does each person and each group think of itself as virtuous and the other as evil? In earlier generations in America, there was a sensitivity to this problem, taught by the churches. Abraham Lincoln, a profound theological thinker, was keenly aware of the tendency of warring parties always to think of themselves as righteous and godly, excusing themselves of all fault. For this reason he refused, in his peerless Second Inaugural Address, to blame the South or to gloat over the impending victory of the North.[6]

Saint Paul taught that all people, regardless of their group or religion, are prisoners of Sin. "None is righteous," he wrote. "There is no distinction; . . . all have

6. See Ronald White's fine book, *Lincoln's Greatest Speech* (New York: Simon & Schuster, 2002).

---

sinned . . ." (Rom. 3:22-23). And following that, he wrote, "God has *consigned all human beings* to disobedience, that he may have *mercy upon all*" (Rom. 11:32, emphasis added). Paul, meditating upon the accursed death of Jesus, forsaken on the Cross by God and men, came to the conclusion that it was *the curse itself* that lay at the heart of "the awful way he died." Nothing else could explain the shame and horror of it. If crucifixion was the most accursed of all deaths, then that must have been God's intention all along.

On the Cross, Jesus voluntarily and willingly bowed his head under the power of Sin and the curse of God. It is vital that we understand that the Father did not do this to the Son; the Son and the Father are doing this together. Jesus "gives himself with his own hand," as one of our most important Eucharistic hymns says.[7] God is submitting to God's own wrath. That is one of the most important reasons — perhaps the most important reason — that Jesus was crucified. No other mode of execution would have been commensurate with the enormity of the dark Powers holding us in bondage. Jesus' situation

7. "Now, My Tongue, the Mystery Telling," attributed to Saint Thomas Aquinas.

under the harsh judgment of Rome was analogous to our situation under Sin. He was condemned; he was rendered helpless and powerless; he was stripped of his humanity; he was reduced to the status of a beast, declared unfit to live and deserving of a death proper to slaves — and what were we if not slaves? The key passage here is Romans 6:16-18: "You are slaves of the one whom you obey, either of sin, which leads to death, or of obedience, which leads to righteousness. . . . But thanks be to God, that you . . . having been set free from sin, have become slaves of righteousness." This is what happened on the Cross. The Son of God took our place under the dictatorship of Sin. He was condemned by the Law and subject to Death because only he, the Perfectly Righteous One, could break the hold of these Powers and bring us out of our slavery to sin into the service of his righteousness.

And so we see that Jesus Christ exchanged God for Godlessness. His human nature absorbed the curse of the Law, the sentence that deals death to the human being (Rom. 7:11). In one of his most remarkable statements, Paul wrote, "God made him [Christ] to be sin who knew no sin" (2 Cor. 5:21). This is a difficult saying. How could the Son of God "be sin"? Paul sets Jesus' sin*lessness* ("he knew no sin") over against "God made him to be sin" and brings the two phrases together in order to heighten the shock of what is being said. *He knew no sin; he was made sin.* No one can fully understand the depth of this saying of Paul. It is at best a hint. But we can say this much: Whatever it was that was going on that day two thousand years ago, it was as intimately connected to the state of your soul as if it were happening now. When you have finished reading these words, as soon you go on to your next activity you will have already failed in some way to live up to the full picture of the righteousness of God. You will already be making distinctions in your mind between people that are and are not worthy of your attention. Sin has a grip on you that you cannot break. Only the power of God is greater than the power of Sin. In the Cross of Christ he has broken it. Now we are being remade, in spite of our worst selves, into his image. May God grant that this very day you might reach out to some person or group that needs a helping hand from a fellow human being — and in so doing, you will recognize the power of his Cross.

Emptying himself of his divinity (Phil. 2:7-8), Christ allied himself with us in our farthest extremity. The full weight of our enmity with God fell on him. No wonder he cried on the Cross, *My God, my God, why hast thou for-*

saken me? His derelict condition was a direct result of his complete identification with us. The following hymn, "Ah, Holy Jesus," is one of the most profound in all the church's repertoire. In this hymn, the people of God give up all pretense to self-righteousness and admit that we ourselves are the ones responsible for Christ's Crucifixion. The hymn says that "the slave has sinned, and the Son has suffered." We are the slaves — slaves of Sin — and the Son of God is suffering in our place — "for our atonement." Reading, singing, or saying this hymn as a prayer, with careful attention to the words, can be a powerful act of submission to God, on Good Friday or any day. "'Twas I, Lord Jesus, I it was denied thee: I crucified thee."

Let us give ourselves up to the contemplation of this unique story. God the Creator, in the person of his Son, has put himself into our place and made himself to be his own sacrifice. *Christ redeemed us from the curse of the law, having become a curse for us.*

*   *   *

Ah, holy Jesus, how hast thou offended,
That man to judge thee hath in hate pretended?

By foes derided, by thine own rejected,
O most afflicted.

Who was the guilty? Who brought this upon thee?
Alas, my treason, Jesus, hath undone thee.
'Twas I, Lord Jesus, I it was denied thee:
I crucified thee.

Lo, the Good Shepherd for the sheep is offered;
The slave hath sinnèd, and the Son hath suffered;
For our atonement, while we nothing heeded,
God interceded.

For me, kind Jesus, was thy incarnation,
Thy mortal sorrow, and thy life's oblation;
Thy death of anguish and thy bitter passion,
For my salvation.[8]

FOURTH MEDITATION

8. Hymn 158 (Episcopal *Hymnal 1982*), "Ah, Holy Jesus, How Hast Thou Offended," words by Johann Heermann (1585-1647), translated by Robert Seymour Bridges (1844-1930).

⊰⊱ FIFTH MEDITATION ⊰⊱

"I thirst"

After this Jesus, knowing that all was now finished, said (to fulfil the scripture), "I thirst." A bowl full of vinegar stood there; so they put a sponge full of the vinegar on hyssop and held it to his mouth.

JOHN 19:28-29

The degree of thirst suffered by crucified victims must have been indescribable. This is one of many aspects of crucifixion that we of the affluent "first world" are not able to imagine, since very few of us have ever experienced extreme thirst. John's Gospel records that our Lord said from the Cross, just before he died, "I thirst," or "I am thirsty." When I was younger, I heard many Good Friday sermons about this. It was generally said that this cry from the Cross shows Jesus' human vulnerability and his suffering. That is true, of course, but that is not what these words mean in the Fourth Gospel. The Cry of Dereliction in Matthew and Mark is the saying that reveals the Lord's intensity of suffering and his radical vulnerability. John's purpose is different. Each of the three sayings from the Cross in John's Gospel shows Jesus in command, accomplishing God's purposes and dying victorious. So let us take another look at the fifth saying as it is placed within the plan of the Fourth Evangelist.

It is very difficult to tell what exactly was intended by the offering of vinegary wine (*oxos*) to Jesus. It could have been intended as a narcotic to relieve him, or it could have been a hostile gesture to increase his suffering. Scholars who have studied this thoroughly have not been able to come to any firm conclusion. Each of the Four Gospels tells about the wine in a different way. In John, however, the significance of the thirst and the wine is clear. Only John has this saying, and he has left no doubt of the meaning. Let us look carefully at the saying in its context: "After this, Jesus, knowing that all was now finished, said (to fulfil the scripture), 'I thirst'" (John 19:28).

What scripture is he fulfilling? Much discussion surrounds this subject. Many have suggested a verse from Psalm 22, which is often read in unison on Good Friday. Indeed, it could almost be called the crucifixion psalm. It has many passages that are used in the Passion narratives to show the relation of Christ's Crucifixion to Scripture. It begins with the words "My God, my God, why hast thou forsaken me?" and continues like this:

> But I am a worm, and no man;
>   scorned by men, and despised by the people.
> All who see me mock at me. . . .
> "He committed his cause to the LORD; let him
>   deliver him;
> let him rescue him, for he delights in him!"

You can see for yourself how much this sounds like the scenes of the Crucifixion. Many of you will recognize some of it as set to music by Handel in the Good Friday section of the *Messiah*. It continues:

A company of evildoers encircle me;
    they have pierced my hands and feet —
I can count all my bones —
    they stare and gloat over me;
they divide my garments among them,
    and for my raiment they cast lots.

These particular verses play an important part in the narrative of the Gospels. All four Evangelists mention the dividing of garments and the casting of lots, but John goes to extra trouble to show how the psalm is fulfilled in these actions. The purpose is to show that the Crucifixion was planned in the mind of God from the beginning. In John, and to some extent in Luke also, Jesus is not only aware of this fulfillment of Scripture; he is also consciously enacting it even from the Cross. So when he says "I thirst," John explains that he says it "knowing that all was now finished ([and] to fulfil the scripture)."

Psalm 22 contains these words:

My strength is dried up like a potsherd
    [like baked clay],
    and my tongue cleaves to my jaws;
    thou dost lay me in the dust of death.

———

In John's Gospel, therefore, when the Lord Jesus says "I thirst," he is speaking in this case not from his very real mortal weakness, but from his sovereign control of his own mission. This is the Son of God speaking, the Second Person of the Blessed Trinity. Even in the midst of his helpless condition, he is manifestly aware of his divine destiny. This is the way that John has portrayed the Lord throughout his narrative, from beginning to end. In chapter 10, Jesus says, "I lay down my life for [my] sheep. . . . No one takes it from me, but I lay it down of my own accord. I have power to lay it down, and I have power to take it again; this charge I have received from my Father" (John 10:15, 18). The Crucifixion is not an accident, not a mistake, not an unfortunate slip-up. It is the deliberate self-offering of the Good Shepherd. And so when he says "I thirst," it is to show that he is fulfilling his purpose according to the plan of God from the beginning.

Now, having noted the lofty purpose of John's Gospel, we may pause to think about the thirst itself. Let us look back to the beginning of the Gospel, to the story of the Samaritan woman at the well. You will perhaps remember her circumstances. She is a person of dubious reputation who comes to draw water alone in the heat of the day so as to avoid the disapproval of the other women who come and socialize in the evening. The Samaritan woman and our Lord have a memorable conversation at the well. He has no container, so when she approaches, he asks her to let him drink from her jar. "The Samaritan woman said to him, 'How is it that you, a Jew, ask a drink of me, a woman of Samaria?' For Jews have no dealings with Samaritans" (John 4:9). This woman has an extra disadvantage: not only is her personal life disorderly, but she is also a member of a despised group. Her meeting with our Lord is therefore doubly significant. Notice now what follows. Everything that has been said so far is on the level of actual water, actual drinking. Now Jesus raises the level of the dialogue:

> Jesus answered her, "If you knew the gift of God, and who it is that is saying to you, 'Give me a drink,' you would have asked him, and he would have given you living water." The woman said to him, "Sir, you have nothing to draw with, and the well is deep; where do you get that living water?" ... Jesus said to her, "... whoever drinks of the water that I shall give ... *will never thirst;* the water that I shall give ... will become in [that person] *a spring of water welling up to eternal life.*" (vv. 10-11, 13-14; emphasis added)

All through the Old Testament, God the Creator is praised as the One who commands the waters. He is the One who sets their boundaries and causes them to flow in courses that he has laid. He makes it rain for forty days and then calls the floods back into their beds and streams. He piles up the waters of the Red Sea on the right hand and on the left so that the children of Israel can pass through. He makes water gush from a barren rock for his people to drink in the wilderness. He withholds the rain for three years and then sends it once again at his prophet Elijah's word. In the "thunderstorm psalm," we read,

> The voice of the Lord is upon the waters;
> the God of glory thunders,
> the Lord, upon many waters. . . .
> The Lord sits enthroned over the flood. . . .
>
> (Ps. 29:3, 10)

This mighty Creator God is the same that John's Gospel identifies at the outset: "In the beginning was the Word. . . . *All things were made through him* . . . and the Word was made flesh and dwelt among us" (John 1:1, 3, 14). Jesus Christ, therefore — the Word made flesh — is the same

One who commands *living water,* the *water that wells up to eternal life.* Following this promise to the Samaritan woman, in chapter 7 he stands up in the temple and proclaims to all who are gathered there, "If anyone thirst, let him come to me and drink. He who believes in me, as the scripture has said, 'Out of his heart shall flow rivers of living water'" (John 7:37-38).

Reflect now upon the saying from the Cross, *I thirst,* and compare it to the saying *Whoever drinks of the water that I shall give will never thirst,* and to the saying *If anyone thirst, let him come to me and drink.* The meaning is almost too staggering to absorb. This three-hour service offers us the opportunity to approach it in solemn contemplation. The One who gives the calm of lakes and pools, the freshness of brooks and streams, the majestic depths of seas and oceans, the glory of pounding surf, the might of Niagara and the tinkle of the garden fountain, the One from whose being flows the gift of the water of eternal life — this is the One who is dying of a terrible thirst on the Cross for the love of his lost sheep.

*　　*　　*

Sing, my tongue, the glorious battle; of the mighty
    conflict sing;
Tell the triumph of the victim, to his cross thy tribute bring.
Jesus Christ, the world's Redeemer, from that cross
    now reigns as King.

Thirty years among us dwelling, his appointed
    time fulfilled,
Born for this, he meets his passion, this the Savior
    freely willed:
On the cross the Lamb is lifted, where his precious blood
    is spilled.

He endures the nails, the spitting, vinegar, and spear,
    and reed;
From that holy Body broken blood and water forth proceed:
Earth, and stars, and sky, and ocean, by that flood
    from stain are freed.[1]

FIFTH MEDITATION

1. Hymn 165 (Episcopal *Hymnal 1982*), "Sing, My Tongue, the Glorious Battle," words by Venantius Honorius Fortunatus (540?-600?); version *Hymnal 1982*, after John Mason Neale (1818-1866).

"It is finished"

The passage we just examined from the Gospel of John continues:

A bowl full of vinegar stood there; so they
put a sponge full of the vinegar on hyssop
and held it to his mouth. When Jesus had
received the vinegar, he said, "It is finished";
and he bowed his head and gave up his spirit.

JOHN 19:29-30

Those who have read thus far will be aware that the Fourth Evangelist (John) has carefully crafted a progression of three sayings. First, Jesus gives his mother to the Beloved Disciple, creating the new community that will bear his Spirit into the world after he has returned to the Father. Next, John seems to be saying that this final action completes the Lord's work, for the verse after that reads, "Jesus, knowing that all was now finished, said (to fulfil the scripture), 'I thirst.'" The soldiers put the vinegary wine on a sponge, and he takes it, in fulfillment of Psalm 69:21:

For my thirst they gave me vinegar to drink.

Finally, John tells us, "When Jesus had received the vinegar, he said, 'It is finished'; and he bowed his head and gave up his spirit."

Now we need to ask further about the meaning of "It is finished." The English is ambiguous, but the Greek is not. It does not mean "It's over; this is the end; I'm done for." It means "It is completed; it is perfected." The Latin says it splendidly: *Consummatum est*. Jesus is announcing that, at the precise moment when he seems to be defeated, he is actually the conqueror: *Christus Victor*. He has done what he came into the world to do, the Word made flesh. Earlier in John's Gospel, his disciples ask him why he hasn't eaten. He says, *My food is to do the will of him who sent me, and to accomplish his work* (4:34). He now announces, "It is accomplished."

And so the One who drinks sour wine as he dies is the very One who said, "I am the [grape]vine" (John 15:1). He is the true source of all fruit and life: "I am the vine, you are the branches. . . . I chose you and appointed you that you should go and bear fruit and that your fruit should abide" (John 15:5, 16). The One who is starving on the Cross is the One who said, "I am the bread of life; [the one] who comes to me shall not hunger" (6:35). The man on the Cross who is dying of thirst is the One who said, "Whoever drinks of the water that I shall give him will never thirst" (4:14). The One who is about to enter the citadel of death is the One who said, "I am the resurrection and the life . . . whoever lives and believes in me shall never die" (11:25-26).

All of these things are completed in the Cross of Christ — all these and more. But to see what is completed most of all, perhaps, we should go back to the very beginning of John's Gospel. The purpose of the Lord's sacrifice is laid out there. Twice it is repeated, in rapid succession, as though to focus our attention on it. Twice the appointed witness says it, the man who was sent from God, according to the Prologue of the Gospel, the man who came for testimony to the Light — twice in the first chapter he identifies the purpose of Jesus' life and death. "Behold," says John the Baptist as he sees Jesus coming toward him for the first time. "Behold, the Lamb of God, who takes away the sin of the world!" (John 1:29-36).

In order to understand the full dimensions of Jesus' work of taking away the sin of the world, we may need to look beyond John's Gospel to other portions of the New Testament. There are other texts that comment specifically on the work of Christ as *finished, perfected, accomplished*. There is no aspect of Christian faith more difficult for us to believe. It is in the nature of the human being to think that Christ's work could not possibly be finished, that we have to do more, we have to add to it, we have to earn it. The ending of the movie *Saving Private Ryan* is a good example. The Tom Hanks character, as he dies, says, "Earn this." The final scene shows Private Ryan as an older man, decades later, making a pilgrimage to the grave of the man who died saving him. Ryan collapses in tears, tormented by the idea that he has not earned the sacrifice. A similar thought was voiced not long ago by the Episcopal Bishop of the Armed Forces, a Vietnam veteran who was interviewed by *The New York Times*. He is haunted by the memory of the people he killed. At the end of the interview he says that he hopes he is forgiven, but he is not sure.[1] The bishop has inadvertently hinted at the same thought: that Christ's work is somehow not complete, that we have to do something further in order to earn its benefits.

There was a very affecting story on the front page of *The New York Times* during the Iraq war in 2003. It described the distress of a young corporal from Chicago, a gunner on an Abrams tank that had "Bush and Co." stenciled on its gun barrel. He had killed two civilians by mistake. Members of the families who were preparing the bodies for burial shouted at him, "Is this what you Americans call freedom?" The reporter wrote that the young corporal's face showed "a sadness that was beyond affectation," and he asked for a translator so that he could say something to the families. "Tell them," he said, "tell them the fact that I pulled the trigger that killed some of these

1. Chris Hedges, interview with the Episcopal Bishop of the Armed Forces, *The New York Times*, 20 December 2003.

people makes me very unhappy. Tell them that America did not want things to happen this way. Tell them that I wish that Iraqis will live a better life."[2] I feel sure you will agree that one would have to love this young man.

I am remembering another news story from the first week of the war. The final words in this second story came from an army chaplain. The young men brag among themselves, he said, but then they come to talk to him. "It bothers them to take life," he said. "They want to talk to me so that they know that I know they are not awful human beings."[3]

I am thinking about what well-meaning people will say to the young corporal to make him feel better. Many will say, "You shouldn't feel bad. You didn't do it on purpose. You were afraid they were suicide bombers." And so forth. This is all true, but it won't make this sensitive young man feel any better. Consciously or unconsciously, he knows in his heart that even unintended actions have consequences. The book of Leviticus, in the

2. John F. Burns, "G.I. Who Pulled the Trigger Shares Anguish of Two Deaths," *The New York Times,* 12 April 2003.

3. Steven Lee Myers, "Haunting Thoughts After a Fierce Battle," *The New York Times,* 27 March 2003.

Old Testament, is the place to look to learn about this. Chapters 4 and 5 of this book are filled with directions about what to do to gain forgiveness for *unintentional* sins. "The LORD said to Moses, 'If any one sins *unwittingly* in any of the things which the LORD has commanded not to be done . . . then let him bring an animal without blemish for a sin offering . . . and the priest shall take some of the blood of the sin offering and . . . make atonement for him for the sin which he has committed, and he shall be forgiven'" (emphasis added).

The trouble with this procedure, as the New Testament letter to the Hebrews makes very clear, is that it had to be done over and over every time there was an unintentional sin. The suggestion in Hebrews is that the sinner could never be free of a sense of unease. Moreover, there was uncertainty about whether this really was sufficient. Could the blood of bulls and lambs really take away sin? The message of the letter is that it could not:

It [the law about sacrifices for atonement] can never, by the same sacrifices which are continually offered year after year, make perfect those who draw near. Otherwise, would they not have ceased to be offered? If the worshipers had once been cleansed, they would no longer have any consciousness of sin. But in these sacrifices there is a reminder of sin year after year. For it is impossible that the blood of bulls and goats should take away sins. (Heb. 10:1-4)

The animal sacrifices of the Old Testament were an imperfect method. They were "only a shadow of the good things to come instead of the true form of these realities" (Heb. 10:1). These rituals were ordained by God in order to prepare his people to understand the perfect and complete sacrifice for sin that was yet to come: "Behold, the Lamb of God, who takes away the sin of the world."

We cannot earn God's gifts of forgiveness, reconciliation, resurrection, and eternal life. These divine gifts are beyond our capacity to earn through any means we could possibly devise. It has already been done for us. It is freely accomplished through the self-giving of Christ. He is the perfect sin offering, "once for all" (*ephapax*), as the letter to the Hebrews repeatedly says (7:27; 9:12; 9:26; 10:10). That is the message for that young corporal and for the bishop and for each and every one of us. Only the death by crucifixion of the Son of God was sufficient to lift the terrible curse of sin from the world. The hymn that comes next speaks of his "manifold disgrace." Nothing less than that would suffice. The ugliness of his Crucifixion corresponds to the ugliness of the sin of the world. He has passed through his ordeal "out of bondage into freedom, out of sin into righteousness, out of death into life." *It is finished.* It is accomplished. It is enough. It is *once — for all.*

*   *   *

I love thee, Lord, but not because I hope for heaven thereby,
Nor yet for fear that loving not I might for ever die,
But for that thou didst all the world upon the
        cross embrace,
For us didst bear the nails and spear, and
        manifold disgrace,
And griefs and torments numberless, and sweat of agony;
E'en death itself; and all for one who was thine enemy.

Then why, most loving Jesus Christ, should I not
        love thee well,
Not for the sake of winning heav'n, nor any fear of hell,
Not with the hope of gaining aught, not seeking a reward,
But as thyself hast lovèd me, O ever-loving Lord!

———

E'en so I love thee, and will love, and in thy praise
    will sing,
Solely because thou art my God and my eternal King.[4]

SIXTH MEDITATION

4. Hymn 682 (Episcopal *Hymnal 1982*), "I Love Thee, Lord, But Not Because I Hope for Heaven Thereby," Spanish lyrics, 17th century; translated by Edward Caswall (1814-1878), adapted by Percy Dearmer (1867-1936), alt. Copyright © 1925 Oxford University Press. Used by permission. All rights reserved.

"Father, into thy hands
I commend my spirit"

It was now about the sixth hour, and there
was darkness over the whole land until the
ninth hour, while the sun's light failed; and
the curtain of the temple was torn in two.
Then Jesus, crying with a loud voice, said,
"Father, into thy hands I commit my spirit!"
And having said this he breathed his last.

LUKE 23:44-46

All four Evangelists tell us that the crucified Messiah quoted from the Psalms. The Psalms have always been the foundation for Jewish and Christian prayer. Somewhere in the world at every minute of the day, someone is saying a psalm. When you pray the Psalms, you are praying with the patriarchs and matriarchs, the prophets and the apostles, the angels and archangels and all the company of heaven. Most of all, you are praying with Jesus himself. The final saying in Luke's Gospel is a direct quotation from Psalm 31:5, "Into thy hand I commit my spirit," with the addition of the address to the Father. Luke continues, "And having said this he breathed his last." The traditional way of lining up the Seven Last Words is to have our Lord declaring that "it is finished," as he does in John, and then, finally, committing himself to his Father, as he does in Luke.

We should not oversentimentalize the Gospel of Luke. It is true that he softens many of the details that he takes over from Mark. It is true also that Luke is beloved for the Christmas story and the other stories he tells that none of the other Evangelists do: the Lost Sheep, the Prodigal Son, the Good Samaritan, Mary and Martha, the Widow's Mite, the Road to Emmaus. But the Gospel of Luke also has an apocalyptic note. It is Luke who tells us that when Jesus was victorious over the Devil after the Temptation in the wilderness, the Devil "departed from him *until an opportune time*" (4:13, emphasis added). That opportune time, it appears, was just after the Last Supper, when the disciples accompanied the Master to the Mount of Olives. There, in the Garden of Gethsemane, Jesus experienced his agony just prior to his arrest. When Jesus is seized in the Garden, he says to those who have come out against him, "This is your hour, and the power of darkness" (22:53). In other words, it is the Devil's hour. When our Lord rises from his knees in the Garden, he rises as one who is preparing to enter the conflict decreed for him from the beginning — preparing to engage the ancient Enemy *mano a mano*. In John's Gospel, this is stated clearly in the words of Jesus as he turns toward his Passion: "Now is the judgment of this world, now shall the ruler of this world be cast out" (12:31). It is the battle for the salvation of the world.

We are not to think of Jesus slipping delicately from the Cross into a golden twilight. The cost of forgiving one's tormentors is huge. *Father, forgive them, for they know not what they do* is a battle in itself. I remember reading a letter to the editor after the Columbine High School massacre. The writer was objecting to the way that the Christian leaders in the local churches were asking the students to forgive the killers before the blood was even dry. This letter-writer protested, "Forgiveness is hard work!" You had the feeling she knew what she was talking about from personal experience.

So even Luke envisions Jesus waging a battle on the Cross. The whole business of the two thieves dramatizes the intensity of his struggle to absorb into himself the malice of those who were reviling him, while at the same time turning his attention toward the one who was looking for a word of redemption. Jesus, in his death as in his life, was entirely directed to the ultimate welfare of others. His entire ministry was directed outward from himself. The kinds of things that preoccupy you and me apparently did not enter his mind. Things like, how am I doing, did I get enough praise today, does that person appreciate me, is that other person over there getting ahead of me, am I slipping behind, am I letting people walk over me — these kinds of things had no hold on him. He was so utterly secure in himself that he was free for others in a way we can scarcely imagine. Therefore, it is exactly in character for him even in the midst of his agony to be mindful of the criminal hanging nearby. Such a thing appears to have been in his nature. What brought him to

---

his knees, what caused him to sweat blood and pray with great intensity, was the thought of the battle he was to fight with the Power of darkness on the Cross.

Earlier he had said to his disciples, "As the lightning flashes and lights up the sky from one side to the other, so will be the coming of the Son of Man. But first he must suffer many things and be rejected" (Luke 17:24-25). His triumph would be won, but only at greatest cost. Another time, he said to the disciples, "I saw Satan fall like lightning from heaven" (Luke 10:18), so we know that he had before him the vision of his victory; but it would come only through his suffering. Once, we are told, "while they were all marveling" at the wonderful things he did — the healings and exorcisms and miracles — he turned to them and said, "Let these words sink into your ears; for the Son of Man is to be delivered into the hands of [wicked] men" (Luke 9:44), but they could not believe it; it was completely outside anyone's conception of the Messiah that he would be betrayed, condemned, and crucified.

Here in this final portion of our Good Friday vigil, we are trying to gain some deeper understanding of what this all means for us personally. In preparing to examine more closely the final saying, "Father, into thy hands I commit my spirit," I have tried to indicate that not even Saint Luke would have us believe that this offering of Christ's life was a gentle passage into a heavenly reward. In these meditations I have written first of John's and now of Luke's three sayings separately from the others so that we can see how they fit into the purposes of these two Evangelists, but in the end the Christian tradition has always combined the seven sayings into a whole. When I was in seminary, I had many wonderful professors, but in recent years there is one, a theologian, who has emerged as the most prominent in my memory. He is long dead now, but I will never forget what he meant to me. I remember in particular talking to him once about great questions of life and death, and the struggle to believe and to make sense of things. His only child, a son, had been born when he and his wife were in their forties, and then they lost him to a rare disease when he was twenty-three. Out of his great grief, this bereaved father said, "The Christian life is lived in between — in between *My God, my God, why hast thou forsaken me?* and *Father, into thy hands I commend my spirit.*"

So in this last saying from the Cross, Luke is teaching us how to die and how to live. Because we, by faith, are assimilated to Christ in his death, we also are assimilated to him in his life beyond death. In his suffering we find our redemption. In his abandonment we find our acceptance. In his dereliction we find our salvation. And at last we are able to say even in the midst of doubt and perplexity, *Father, into thy hands I commend my spirit,* even as the Lord and Savior Jesus Christ said.

This word, *Father:* What can we say about it? Not everyone has had a father who showed forth the fatherly love and care which Jesus knew. Some would want to substitute "Mother." But as we know from many Scripture references, the concept of a loving, protecting, nurturing Father embraces the image of a mother also. We call God "Father" because Jesus did, and I confess that is enough for me. It means that we are related to God as a beloved child, one for whose welfare the parent pours himself out day by day. We know virtually nothing of Saint Joseph, but he must have given the young boy Jesus some idea of what a strong, tender father was like. Through his early experience of father and mother, the child Jesus was enabled to put his trust in the One Father in heaven — the Father whom he would know so well at the age of twelve that he would be able precociously to say, "Did you not know that I must be about my Father's business?" (Luke 2:49) — as indeed he was, all the way to the final, dreadful, unthinkable moment, still trusting: *Father, into thy hands I commend my spirit.* A perfect life lived, a terrible death died, all for the sake of bringing you and me into the near presence of that same Father forever, with him.

I found some words in a Good Friday sermon by Alexander Maclaren, one of the great preachers of the late nineteenth century. They express what I want to say to you today. Maclaren said, "My words, I feel, in this sermon, have been very poor; but poor as they have been, if you have listened to them, you will not be exactly the same [person] as you were before." Anyone who has read this far has stayed with our Lord on the Cross for some special reason. The Father of Jesus has his hand on you in some way. You can trust that. Even as you read, you can give yourself up in this hour to the prayer of our Redeemer and commit yourself to our Father through him. The next hymn can enable you to do that. Four times the refrain is repeated: *Thou didst give thyself for me/Now I give myself to thee.* You can make these words your own in this very hour. Your crucified Lord holds out his arms to you in the love that will not let you go.

*   *   *

Let thy Blood in mercy poured,
Let thy gracious Body broken
Be to me, O gracious Lord,
Of thy boundless love the token.
Thou didst give thyself for me,
Now I give myself to thee.

Thou didst die that I might live;
Blessed Lord, thou cam'st to save me;
All that love of God could give
Jesus by his sorrows gave me.
Thou didst give thyself for me,
Now I give myself to thee.

By the thorns that crowned thy brow,
By the spear-wound and the nailing,
By the pain and death, I now
Claim, O Christ, thy love unfailing.
Thou didst give thyself for me,
Now I give myself to thee.

Wilt thou own the gift I bring?
All my penitence I give thee;
Thou art my exalted King;
of thy matchless love forgive me.
Thou didst give thyself for me,
Now I give myself to thee.[1]

AMEN

1. Hymn 313 (Episcopal *Hymnal 1982*), "Let Thy Blood in Mercy Poured," words by John Brownlie (1859-1925).

———

81